No Fuss Low Carb One Pot Meals

Easy and Healthy Everyday Recipes

Sarah Spencer

Copyrights

All rights reserved © 2018 by Sarah Spencer and The Cookbook Publisher. No part of this publication or the information in it may be quoted from or reproduced in any form by means such as printing, scanning, photocopying, or otherwise without prior written permission of the copyright holder.

Disclaimer and Terms of Use

Effort has been made to ensure that the information in this book is accurate and complete. However, the author and the publisher do not warrant the accuracy of the information, text, and graphics contained within the book due to the rapidly changing nature of science, research, known and unknown facts, and internet. The author and the publisher do not hold any responsibility for errors, omissions, or contrary interpretation of the subject matter herein.

The recipes provided in this book are for informational purposes only and are not intended to provide dietary advice. A medical practitioner should be consulted before making any changes in diet. Additionally, recipe cooking times may require adjustment depending on age and quality of appliances. Readers are strongly urged to take all precautions to ensure ingredients are fully cooked to avoid the dangers of foodborne illnesses. The nutritional information for recipes contained in this book are provided for informational purposes only. This information is based on the specific brands, ingredients, and measurements used to make the recipe and therefore the nutritional information is an estimate, and in no way is intended to be a guarantee of the actual nutritional value of the recipe made in the reader's home. The author and the publisher will not be responsible for any damages resulting in your reliance on the nutritional information. The best method to obtain an accurate count of the nutritional value in the recipe is to calculate the information with your specific brands, ingredients, and measurements. The recipes and suggestions provided in this book are solely the opinion of the author. The author and publisher do not take any responsibility for any consequences that may result due to following the instructions provided in this book.

ISBN: 9781728882482

Printed in the United States

Contents

Introduction _____ 1

Chicken & Poultry _____ 3

Beef _____ 17

Pork & Lamb _____ 29

Fish & Seafood _____ 39

Vegetarian _____ 51

Desserts _____ 59

Recipe Index _____ 67

Also by Sarah Spencer _____ 69

Appendix - Cooking Conversion Charts _____ 71

Introduction

So, you want to watch your carbs. Well, this book contains recipes that are perfect for the person who wants meals that are easy to prepare and low in carbohydrates. **In fact, all of the recipes you will find here have eight grams of carbs or less**. This is ideal for a ketogenic diet, but it's also useful for the person who just wants to eat healthier. The recipes here don't focus on being low calorie or low fat; most of them actually have significant fat content and more than a few calories. (But not all of them!) and the best part is that you will use only one pot to prepare delicious dishes your family and friends will enjoy.

Studies show that fat is essential to your health. Carbs, on the other hand, are not. Carbs have the biggest impact on your body's insulin levels as they turn to sugars once they are consumed. This can lead to overeating, diabetes, dementia, cancer, and cardiovascular diseases. Low carb diets lower triglycerides while increasing HDL or "good cholesterol".

Reducing the carbs in your diet is a fantastic way to up your energy and even drop those excess pounds, both of which will leave you feeling and looking phenomenal all day. However, one of the challenges many people face while sticking to a low-carb eating plan is the meal planning required. You can't simply slap something between two pieces of bread and go. No, eating low-carb means thinking about the combination of things you are putting in your body. You actually have to prep, chop, and prepare if you are determined to obtain that slim, healthy body you've always wanted.

And it doesn't matter if you've had a long day and are feeling about as energetic as a snail. You need to eat, and that's when people go astray either ordering carb- and preservative-dripping take-out or whipping up something quick and easy like pasta or a sandwich.

We are pleased to share with you a third option that's going to help you eat delicious low-carb meals without any fuss. Welcome to your low-carb one-pot meal cookbook, which includes recipes you can make using only pot, dish, or bowl and then forget about it while you take a load off.

The key to low-carb eating is limiting your sugars and carbohydrates so your body goes into a ketogenic state, which means it burns up the fat stocks in your body like nobody's business. In order to get your body into that ketogenic state, you need to stop eating simple carbohydrates and replace them with lots of veggies and proteins like meats and nuts.

Processed foods should be avoided since they contain all sorts of hidden dangers including high levels of sugars and carbs. Dairy products can be enjoyed but should make up a smaller portion of your diet than veggies and proteins.

The recipes you will find here are full of protein and the good dietary fat that will leave you feeling full and happy. Several of the recipes call for an Instant Pot or slow cooker, but they can easily be prepared using the stovetop or the oven if you'd prefer.

Chicken & Poultry

Chicken and Veggies

This super easy chicken and vegetable sheet pan supper is healthy and nutritious, containing only 6.4g total carbs. You can't go wrong with this meal!

Serves 4 | Prep. time 5 minutes | Cooking time 15 minutes

Ingredients
4 medium chicken breasts, diced
2 large bell peppers, diced (any color(s) you like)
1 onion, diced
2 zucchinis, diced
2 cups broccoli florets
1 cup fresh diced tomatoes, plum or grape
¼ cup olive oil
1 teaspoon salt
1 teaspoon black pepper
2 teaspoons Italian seasoning
½ teaspoon paprika

Directions
1. Preheat oven to 425°F.
2. Place all the meat and veggies on a nonstick baking tray.
3. Drizzle with olive oil and stir to make sure everything is well coated. Add the seasonings and stir again to distribute.
4. Transfer the tray to the oven and bake for 20-30 minutes or until the chicken is cooked through.
5. Broil for 1-2 minutes for browned

Nutrition (per serving)
Calories 241, fat 15.2g, carbs 6.4 g, protein 19.9g, sodium 357mg

Slow Cooker Chicken and Bacon Chowder

This amazing chicken chowder is a simple one pot "throw it in and forget about it" meal. You can pan sear the chicken breasts before putting them into the slow cooker if you want, but it isn't necessary.

Serves 4–6 | Prep. time 10 minutes | Cooking time 6–8 hours

Ingredients
4 cloves garlic, minced
1 shallot, finely chopped
1 small leek, cleaned, trimmed and sliced
2 ribs celery, diced
6 ounces crimini mushrooms, sliced
1 medium sweet onion, thinly sliced
4 tablespoons butter
2 cups chicken stock
1 pound chicken breasts
8 ounces cream cheese
1 cup heavy cream
1 pound bacon, cooked crisp and crumbled
1 teaspoon sea salt
1 teaspoon black pepper
1 teaspoon garlic powder
1 teaspoon dried thyme

Directions
1. Add everything but the heavy cream to the slow cooker and cook on low for 6–8 hours. Stir once in a while to make sure the cream cheese gets distributed into the sauce.
2. 30 minutes before serving, add the heavy cream and stir. Let cook an additional 30 minutes to heat the cream through and serve.

Nutrition (per serving)
Calories 355, fat 28 g, carbs 6.4g, protein 21g, sodium 612 mg

Chicken Jalapeno Popper Soup

(Pressure Cooker or Instant Pot)

The spicy goodness of Jalapeno Poppers in a soup! With only 5g carbs per serving it is a delicious dinner. There is an extra step if you want the cream cheese topping, but it's worth the few extra minutes.

Serves 4 | Prep. time 3 minutes | Cooking time 20 minutes

Ingredients
½ cup salted butter
2 yellow onions, diced
1½ pounds boneless chicken breasts (about 2-3 breasts), cut into chunks
1 teaspoon ground cumin
2 teaspoons sea salt
1 teaspoon freshly ground black pepper
¼ teaspoon dried oregano
¼ teaspoon paprika
4 large jalapeno peppers, trimmed, seeds and membrane removed, and finely diced
2 cloves garlic, minced
¾ cup heavy cream
2 cups chicken broth
½ cup cream cheese, divided
1 cup extra sharp cheddar cheese, shredded (save a tablespoon for topping)
1 cup Monterey Jack Cheese, shredded (save a tablespoon for topping)

Jalapeno Cream Topper
3 tablespoons cream cheese
¼ cup heavy cream
1 large jalapeno pepper, cleaned and minced

Directions
1. On the Sauté/Browning mode, let the butter melt in the pot and fry the onions for 2-3 minutes until tender.
2. Add garlic and diced jalapenos. Sauté for 2 minutes. Add chicken and brown on all sides. Add remaining ingredients EXCEPT the cream cheese, cheddar cheese, the Monterey Jack cheese, and the ingredients for the jalapeños cream.
3. Cover and lock the lid. Make sure the valve is closed. Set cooker's mode to High pressure and pressure cook for 2 minutes. Let the pressure release naturally for about 10 minutes.
4. Uncover and move chicken to a plate and shred with forks. Add chicken back to the soup. Use the keep warm mode. Add the three cheeses, cover, and let melt for 4-6 minutes. Mix with a wooden spoon to coat well.
5. Mix together the jalapeños cream ingredient. Evenly add a dollop of the jalapeños cream to each bowl and sprinkle with some of the remaining cheddar and Monterey Jack cheeses.

Nutrition (per serving)
Calories 498, fat 38g, carbs 5g, protein 32g, sodium 535mg

Kung Pao Chicken

This easy one-pot version of a classic Asian dish has only 8g carbs. It is so flavorful and aromatic that you will make it again and again.

Serves 4 | Prep. time 15 minutes | Cooking time 12 minutes

Ingredients
Sauce
3 tablespoons coconut aminos or low sodium soy sauce
1 teaspoon fish sauce
2 teaspoons sesame oil
1 teaspoon apple cider vinegar
¼–½ teaspoon red pepper chili flakes to taste
½ teaspoon fresh ginger, minced
2 cloves garlic, minced
2–3 tablespoons water or chicken broth
1–2 teaspoons monk fruit or erythritol (adjust to desired sweetness)

Stir-Fry
¾ pound chicken thighs, cut into 1-inch pieces
Himalayan pink salt and black pepper as needed
3–4 tablespoons olive oil or avocado oil
1 red bell pepper, chopped into bite-sized pieces
1 medium-large zucchini, halved
2–3 dried red chili peppers
⅔ cup roasted cashews or roasted peanuts
Sesame seeds and chopped green onions for garnish (optional)

Directions
1. In a mixing bowl, combine the ingredients for the sauce. Mix well and set aside.
2. Heat oil in a nonstick skillet. Toss in the chicken pieces and cook for about 5 minutes or until the chicken is almost cooked through.
3. Add the zucchini, both kinds of peppers, salt, and pepper and cook a couple of minutes longer. Then add the sauce and cook until the sauce starts to reduce.
4. You can add a little cornstarch slurry to thicken the sauce if you want.

Nutrition (per serving)
Calories 415, fat 30 g, carbs 8 g, protein 18 g, sodium 714 mg

Chicken Marsala

This delicious dish is cooked in one skillet and has only 6g carbs per serving. The wine adds a rich flavor that will have your taste buds dancing.

Serves 4 | Prep. time 10 minutes | Cooking time 10–20 minutes

Ingredients
4 boneless skinless chicken breast cutlets, pounded thin
1 small onion, chopped
1 cup crimini mushrooms, sliced
3 tablespoons olive oil
½ cup dry Marsala wine
2 tablespoons minced Italian (flat-leaf) parsley
½ cup chicken broth
2 cups broccoli

Directions
1. In a skillet, heat the olive oil. When hot, add chicken and cook for about 5 minutes on each side.
2. If you pounded the chicken thin, you can remove it now. Otherwise, you can leave it in when you add the vegetables.
3. Add the chopped onion, mushrooms and broccoli and cook until soft.
4. Add the wine and cook for 2 minutes. If you need more liquid, add the chicken broth as needed.
5. Return the chicken to the skillet if you took it out.
6. Serve the chicken with vegetables and sauce.

Nutrition (per serving)
Calories 255, fat 14 g, carbs 4 g, protein 27 g, sodium 118 mg

White Chicken Chili

You will love this chicken chili with its kick of spice and creaminess combined with the fact that it has only 6g of carbs per serving.

Serves 4 | Prep. time 5 minutes | Cooking time 8 hours

Ingredients
2 pounds chicken breasts
2 teaspoons chili powder
1 teaspoon cumin
1 teaspoon garlic powder
½ cup chicken broth
9 ounces (2 4½-ounce cans) chopped green chilies, drained
3 tablespoons butter
½ cup heavy cream
½ cup cream cheese
½ cup sour cream
Toppings (if desired)
⅓ cup chopped cilantro
⅓ cup red onion, peeled and chopped
1 cup Pepper Jack cheese, shredded

Directions
1. Add all ingredients to the slow cooker except for the butter, cream, cream cheese, and sour cream.
2. Cook for 6–7 hours.
3. An hour before serving, mix together the butter, cream cheese, cream, and sour cream until smooth.
4. Add the cream mixture to the slow cooker and cook an hour longer.
5. Serve with additional sour cream if desired.

Nutrition (per serving)
Calories 486, fat 33 g, carbs 6 g, protein 39 g, sodium 592 mg

Chicken Cordon Bleu Casserole

This easy casserole is simple to throw together and bake. With only 4g carbs per serving, it is a perfect choice for a low carb diet, and it makes enough to freeze or to have for lunch the next day.

Serves 12 | Prep. time 15 minutes | Cooking time 40 minutes

Ingredients
1 head cauliflower, cut into florets
¼ cup avocado oil
Sea salt
Black pepper
⅓ cup heavy cream
½ cup sour cream
2 tablespoons Dijon mustard
2 cloves garlic, minced
1½ pounds cooked chicken breast, shredded (weight after cooking)
12 ounces deli ham slices, chopped
2 cups Swiss cheese, shredded (divided)
¼ cup pork rinds, crushed like bread crumbs (optional; measure after crushing)
Chives, chopped, for garnish (optional)

Directions
1. Preheat oven to 400°F.
2. Season the cauliflower with salt and pepper.
3. Stir together the cream, sour cream, mustard, garlic and 1 cup of cheese.
4. Put everything in a casserole dish and top with the remaining cheese.

5. If you choose to use the pork rinds, sprinkle them on top of the casserole and bake for 10 minutes or until it is golden brown and bubbly.
6. Garnish with chives and serve.

Nutrition (per serving)
Calories 304, fat 20 g, carbs 4 g, protein 25 g, sodium 867mg

Bacon Ranch Chicken

Cheesy and loaded with chicken and bacon as well as healthy broccoli. What is there not to love about this low carb recipe?

Serves 4–5 | Prep. time 5 minutes | Cooking time 25 minutes

Ingredients
2 tablespoons butter
1½ tablespoons ranch seasoning mix
½ cup cream cheese, softened to room temperature
¼ cup heavy cream
⅔ cup reduced sodium chicken broth
¼ cup crumbled cooked bacon
½ cup shredded cheese
10.8 ounces frozen broccoli florets, or about 4 cups broccoli
2 cups shredded cooked chicken

Topping
1½ cups shredded cheese
½ cup crumbled cooked bacon

Directions
1. Preheat oven to 350°F.
2. In an ovenproof skillet, melt the butter, then stir in the ranch seasoning, cream cheese, heavy cream, broth, bacon, broccoli, and cheese.
3. When the cheese has all melted, add in the cooked chicken, then sprinkle with additional cheese and transfer to the oven.
4. Bake for about 20 minutes or until hot and bubbly.
5. Serve with extra bacon if desired.

Nutrition (per serving)
Calories 550, fat 43 g, carbs 6 g, protein 35 g, sodium 880 mg

Creamy Spinach Artichoke Chicken

This recipe is both low fat and low carb, and it tastes divine. It has only 5.2g carbs per serving and it is sure to please.

Serves 6 | Prep. time 5 minutes | Cooking time 20 minutes

Ingredients
Cooking spray
6 skinless bone-in chicken thighs (or breast fillets)
1 tablespoon (4 cloves) minced garlic
1 cup reduced fat cream cheese
1 cup chicken stock/broth
1 (14-ounce) can artichoke hearts in brine/water, drained and roughly chopped
4 cups loosely packed baby spinach leaves
Salt to season
¼ cup parmesan cheese

Directions
1. Preheat oven to 400°F.
2. Spray an ovenproof skillet with cooking spray (or use butter) and heat over medium heat.
3. Sprinkle salt and pepper over the chicken thighs to season, then add them (skin side down) to the skillet to sear. Cook for 3 minutes on each side.
4. Stir in garlic and cook about 1 minute, then add in cream cheese and stir until it starts to melt.
5. Add in broth, artichokes, and parmesan cheese. Then add in spinach and transfer to the oven.
6. Bake for 20 minutes.

Nutrition (per serving)
Calories 245, fat 11.2 g, carbs 5.2 g, protein 31.3 g, sodium 403 mg

Sheet Pan Fajitas

When fajitas are this easy to make and have only 6.8g carbs per serving, you will make them a weekly staple. Wrapping them in lettuce leaves instead of tortillas keeps the carbs low.

Serves 6 | Prep. time 10 minutes |cooking time 25 minutes

Ingredients
1 pound chicken breasts, sliced thinly
1 red pepper, sliced
1 green pepper, sliced
1 yellow pepper, sliced
1 onion, halved and sliced
¼ cup olive oil
2 teaspoons chili powder
1 teaspoon cumin
½ teaspoon garlic powder
Pinch of chili flakes
1 teaspoon salt
½ teaspoon ground pepper

Directions
1. Preheat oven to 400°F.
2. Combine the oil, chili powder, cumin, garlic powder and chili flakes in a mixing bowl. Stir together, then toss in the chicken and veggies. Stir to coat.
3. Pour the contents of the bowl onto a nonstick baking sheet and spread out across the sheet.
4. Transfer to the oven and bake for 25 minutes or until the chicken is thoroughly cooked.
5. Serve with lettuce leaves, sour cream, extra cheese, avocado or whatever you enjoy. (The nutritional information is for the chicken and veggies only, though.)

Nutrition (per serving)
Calories 241, fat 16 g, carbs 6.8 g, protein 17 g, sodium 455 mg

Beef

Beef, Spinach and Mozzarella Bake

This super easy one-pot meal is low carb and is good for keto and primal diets. At 7.7g carbs per serving, it is delicious and good for you.

Serves 6 | Prep. time 20 minutes |Cooking time 35 minutes

Ingredients
1 tablespoon extra-virgin olive oil
1½ pounds ground beef
1 small red onion, finely diced
2 garlic cloves, minced
1 teaspoon paprika
1 large red chili pepper, sliced
1 large carrot, diced
1 medium red pepper, diced
1 cup tomatoes, chopped
3½ ounces fresh baby spinach
1 tablespoon tomato puree
2 bay leaves
3 tablespoons chopped fresh parsley
1 tablespoon fresh oregano or 1 teaspoon dried
¼ teaspoon each sea salt and black pepper, or to taste
2 cups chicken stock or beef stock
8 ounces mozzarella cheese, shredded

Directions
1. Preheat oven to 375°F.
2. In a large ovenproof skillet, heat the olive oil over medium heat, then add the ground beef and cook for 5–6 minutes. Drain the fat and return to the stove.

3. Add the carrots, onions, and garlic and sauté for about 4 minutes, then add the pepper, paprika and chili.
4. After that has cooked for a couple of minutes, add the chopped tomatoes, tomato puree, chicken stock, oregano and bay leaves. Cook for approximately 10 more minutes or until the sauce begins to thicken.
5. Top the skillet with shredded cheese and transfer to the oven. Bake for 5–10 minutes or until the cheese is melted and bubbly.

Nutrition (per serving)
Calories 511, fat 36.5 g, carbs 7.7 g, protein 34.5 g, sodium 329 mg

Corned Beef Hash

This is one meal that you can have for breakfast, lunch or dinner. There are no potatoes like traditional hash, but you will never miss them, and at only 7g of carbs per serving, you will love this meal.

Serves 4 | Prep. time 10 minutes | Cooking time 15minutes

Ingredients
2 tablespoons olive oil
1 medium onion, diced
3 cloves garlic, minced
2 cups riced cauliflower (you can do this in your food processor or buy in the produce section of the grocery store)
1 pound corned beef, diced
4 large eggs
2 tablespoons Italian flat leaf parsley, rough chopped
¼ cup sugar-free Russian dressing (optional)

Directions
1. Heat olive oil in a large skillet (cast iron works great).
2. When hot, add the onion and garlic and sauté for 2 minutes.
3. Add the cauliflower and cook, stirring often, until the cauliflower starts to brown nicely.
4. Add the corned beef and cook until it starts to crisp.
5. Make small holes in the corned beef mixture that will fit an egg. Crack an egg into each hole and continue cooking until the eggs are cooked through. (You can cover the skillet to speed this process along, but you may lose some of the crispiness of the corned beef.)
6. Serve with Russian dressing if desired.

Nutrition (per serving)
Calories 422, fat 16g, carbs 5.3 g, protein 36 g, sodium 660 mg

Cheesy Taco Soup

This soup is amazingly delicious and has only 5g carbs per serving. The best part is you can make it as spicy as you want. Perfect for a cold winter night.

Serves 6 | Prep. time 10 minutes | Cooking time 30 minutes

Ingredients
2 pounds ground beef or sausage
1 pound cream cheese
2 (10-ounce) cans of Rotel diced tomatoes (this is where you can add the spice)
1 small onion, diced
2 tablespoons taco seasoning
4 cups chicken broth
¼ cup fresh cilantro
½ cup shredded cheese (for garnish)

Directions
1. Brown the meat in a stockpot over medium heat with the onion.
2. When the beef is browned, add the diced tomatoes, cream cheese, and taco seasoning and stir until the cream cheese is melted.
3. Add the chicken broth and stir. Reduce heat and let cook for 30 minutes.
4. Serve with fresh cilantro and extra cheese.

Nutrition (per serving)
Calories 547, fat 43 g, carbs 5 g, protein 33 g, sodium 724 mg

Instant Pot Beef Bourguignon

This low carb version of the classic dish is low in carbs but still filled with rich flavor. A perfect meal to serve to guests.

Serves 6 | Prep. time 30 minutes | Cooking time 50 minutes

Ingredients
1½–2 pounds beef chuck roast, cut into ¾-inch cubes
5 strips bacon, diced
1 small onion, chopped
10 ounces crimini mushrooms, quartered
2 carrots, chopped
5 cloves garlic, minced
3 bay leaves
¾ cup dry red wine
¾ teaspoon cornstarch
1 tablespoon tomato paste
1 teaspoon dried thyme
Salt and pepper

Directions
1. Season the beef with salt and pepper.
2. Set your Instant Pot to sauté and add the bacon. Cook the bacon for about 5 minutes. When the bacon is browned, drain the grease from the pot and add the beef. Brown the beef evenly on each side, then add the onions and garlic and cook for an additional 3 minutes.
3. Add the red wine and tomato sauce and stir. Make sure to get the brown bits off the bottom.
4. Add the mushrooms, carrots, and thyme. Stir and add the bay leaves.
5. Put the lid on the Instant Pot and seal it securely. Cook on high pressure for 40 minutes. Release the pressure and set the pot on sauté mode again.

6. Mix a slurry with the cornstarch and a bit of water. Add it to the pot and let it boil for a few minutes to thicken.
7. Serve topped with crispy bacon.

Nutrition (per serving)
Calories 220, fat 5 g, carbs 6.5 g, protein 27 g, sodium 310 mg

Stuffed Meatloaf

This stuffed meatloaf is simple and quick to throw together and gives you a full meal in one pot.

8 slices | Prep. time 10 minutes | Cooking time 1 hour

Ingredients
1 pound ground beef or veal
1 teaspoon salt
½ teaspoon pepper
1 teaspoon garlic powder
½ teaspoon cumin
6 slices cheddar cheese
¼ cup onion, diced
¼ cup green onion, diced
½ cup baby spinach
1 cup mushrooms

Directions
1. Preheat oven to 350°F.
2. In a mixing bowl, season the meat with the spices and then divide into two.
3. Press half the meat into a loaf pan, covering the bottom and half the sides.
4. Lay the cheese slices on top of the meat, followed by the onions, spinach, and mushrooms.
5. Cover with the remaining meat and press to connect to the meat on the sides.
6. Bake for 60 minutes.

Nutrition (per serving)
Calories 249, fat 19.6 g, carbs 2 g, protein 15.8 g, sodium 597mg

Slow Cooker Beef Stroganoff

This simple dinner is as easy to assemble as it is delicious. Made in the slow cooker, this is really a "dump it in and forget about it" recipe.

Serves 4 | Prep. time 10 minutes | Cooking time 6 hours

Ingredients
1 onion, sliced and quartered
2 cloves garlic, crushed
2 slices bacon, diced
1⅛ pound beef stewing steak, cubed
1 teaspoon smoked paprika
3 tablespoons tomato paste
1 cup beef stock
8 ounces mushrooms, quartered

Directions
1. Assemble all the ingredients in the slow cooker and stir to combine.
2. Set the slow cooker on low and let cook for 6 hours.
3. Serve with sour cream if desired.

Nutrition (per serving)
Calories 317, fat 19 g, carbs 8 g, protein 29 g, sodium 655 mg

Instant Pot Boneless Short Ribs

This recipe is full of rich flavors but low in carbs. You can make it quickly in the Instant Pot or let it slow cook while you are at work. Versatile and yummy.

Serves 2 | Prep. time 10 minutes | Cooking time 1 hour 10 minutes

Ingredients
2 pounds boneless beef short ribs
1 medium-sized carrot, diced
1 shallot, diced
3 cloves garlic, minced
5 sprigs fresh thyme
½ cup red wine
2 tablespoons balsamic vinegar
1 tablespoon salted butter
½ tablespoon olive oil
Salt and pepper

Directions
1. Season short ribs with salt and pepper.
2. Set the Instant Pot on sauté and add the olive oil and butter. When the Instant Pot is hot, add the short ribs and brown on all sides before removing to a plate.
3. Add the carrots, shallots, and garlic to the Instant Pot and sauté for 3–4 minutes.
4. Turn off the sauté mode, add the red wine and stir. Make sure you get up all the brown bits for added flavor.
5. Return the short ribs to the Instant Pot. Position them along the bottom, and try not to let them overlap. Top with the fresh thyme and add a bit more salt and pepper if you want.

6. Attach the lid securely and cook at high pressure for 45 minutes. Let the pressure naturally release for about 15 minutes, then manually release the rest.
7. Remove the ribs and put the pot back on sauté (you can skim off some of the fat at this point if you want). Add the balsamic vinegar and let boil until the sauce has reduced and thickened.
8. Serve sauce over ribs.

Nutrition (per serving)
Calories 860, fat 51 g, carbs 7 g, protein 88 g, sodium 470 mg

Thai Lettuce Wraps with Veal

These lettuce wraps are flavorful little bites of pure bliss. Cooked in one skillet with only 2g of carbs, you'll want these every night of the week.

Serves 4 | Prep. time 15 minutes | Cooking time 10 minutes

Ingredients
1 tablespoon olive oil
1 pound ground veal
½ cup red cabbage, shredded
½ cup carrots, thinly sliced/julienned
1 small red bell pepper, thinly sliced
1 tablespoon garlic, minced
1 tablespoon fresh ginger, minced
2 teaspoons finely minced lemongrass or lemongrass paste
¼ cup cashews or peanuts, chopped
¼ cup fresh cilantro, chopped
3 green onions, thinly sliced

Sauce
Juice of 1 lime
2 tablespoons Thai red curry paste
1 tablespoon soy sauce
1 teaspoon toasted sesame oil
1–2 teaspoons sriracha (optional, for heat)
16 Bibb lettuce leaves, washed and drained

Directions

1. Make the sauce by mixing the lime juice, soy sauce, red curry paste, sesame oil, and sriracha together in a small bowl.
2. Heat the olive oil in a skillet over medium-high heat. When hot, add the ground veal and cook until browned. Drain off any excess fat.
3. Add the shredded cabbage, carrots, red peppers, garlic, and ginger. Cook for about 4 minutes. You still want the vegetables to have a bit of crunch. Add in the sauce and stir, cooking until it is heated through.
4. Add the chopped nuts, green onions, and cilantro and give it a quick stir.
5. Serve the filling in the lettuce leaves.

Nutrition (per serving)

Calories 73, fat 3 g, carbs 2 g, protein 6 g, sodium 61 mg

Pork & Lamb

Slow Cooked Lamb with Mint and Green Beans

This recipe is perfect for a Sunday dinner with family, an elegant dish that is nutritious, fresh, and healthy that slow cook all day and makes the house smell so good!

Serves 4 | Prep. time 15 minutes | Cooking time 8 hours

Ingredients
1 lamb leg, bone in, about 3 pounds
1 tablespoons olive oil
4 cloves garlic, minced
¼ cup fresh mint leaves
6 cups green beans, trimmed
½ teaspoon salt
½ teaspoon pepper

Directions
1. In a skillet, heat the olive oil and brown the lamb leg on both sides. Transfer to the slow cooker.
2. Place the mint and minced garlic in the slow cooker with the lamb.
3. Cover and cook on LOW for 8–10 hours.
4. Halfway through the cooking time, add the green beans. It's best to remove the lamb, put the beans on the bottom, and then place the lamb back on top of the beans.
5. Finish cooking and serve.

Nutrition (per serving)
Calories 525, fat 36.4 g, carbs 7.6 g, protein 37.3 g, sodium 268 mg

Crock Pot Ham Cauliflower "Potato" Soup

The chowder-like consistency of this soup makes it perfect for an autumn supper. At only 6g carbs per serving, you can enjoy it without guilt.

Serves 6 | Prep. time 5 minutes | Cooking time 4 hours

Ingredients
3 cups diced ham
¼ cup heavy cream
14½ ounces chicken broth
4 cloves garlic
8 ounces cheddar cheese
½ teaspoon garlic powder
½ teaspoon onion powder
½ teaspoon salt
Dash pepper
16-ounce bag frozen cauliflower florets, or a fresh head cut into florets

Directions
1. Mix all the ingredients except the cauliflower in the slow cooker.
2. Cook on HIGH for 4 hours.
3. Add the cauliflower florets and cook for an additional 30 minutes or until the cauliflower is soft.

Nutrition (per serving)
Calories 274, fat 18 g, carbs 6 g, protein 21 g, sodium 1352 mg

Pork Egg Roll in a Bowl

This egg roll in a bowl is super easy to make and it will leave you so satisfied you will never miss the wrapper.

Serves 4 | Prep. time 5 minutes | Cooking time 20 minutes

Ingredients
2 tablespoons sesame oil
3 cloves garlic, minced
½ cup onion, diced
5 green onions, sliced on a bias (white and green parts)
1 pound ground pork
½ teaspoon ground ginger
Sea salt and black pepper to taste
1 tablespoon sriracha or garlic chili sauce
14-ounce bag coleslaw mix
3 tablespoons soy sauce
1 tablespoon rice vinegar
2 tablespoons toasted sesame seeds

Directions
1. In a large skillet, heat the oil over medium-high heat.
2. When the oil is hot, add the onion, garlic and the white part of the green onions. Sauté until the onions are soft and the garlic just begins to brown.
3. Add in the ground pork, ginger, salt, pepper, and sriracha or chili sauce. Cook until the pork is cooked all the way through.
4. Add in the coleslaw mix, rice vinegar, and the soy sauce. Stir to make sure everything has been covered with sauce.
5. Serve in a bowl topped with the sesame seeds and the greens from the green onions.

Nutrition (per serving)
Calories 297, fat 20 g, carbs 7 g, protein 20 g, sodium 457mg

Pizza Frittata

This low carb dinner gives you the amazing pizza flavors without any of the guilt.

Serves 6 | Prep. time 5 minutes | Cooking time 25 minutes

Ingredients
12 eggs
2 cloves garlic, minced
¼ cup pizza sauce
½ cup parmesan cheese, grated
½ cup mozzarella cheese, shredded (divided)
3 ounces Canadian bacon, sliced (divided)
3 ounces pepperoni, sliced (divided)
2 tablespoons olive oil
3 ounces onion, diced (divided)
2 ounces green bell pepper, diced (divided)
2 ounces red bell pepper, diced (divided)
2 ounces mushrooms, thinly sliced (divided)
6 black olives, sliced

Directions
1. Preheat oven to 400°F.
2. In a mixing bowl, whisk the eggs thoroughly.
3. Whisk in the garlic, pizza sauce, parmesan cheese and ¼ cup of the mozzarella cheese.
4. Add half of the Canadian bacon and pepperoni.
5. Heat a large ovenproof skillet over medium to high heat. Add the olive oil and half of each of the onion, bell peppers and mushrooms. Cook until soft.
6. Transfer the egg mixture to the skillet and stir. Move the skillet to the oven and bake for 10 minutes.
7. Top with the remaining ingredients and bake about 7 minutes more.

Nutrition (per serving)
Calories 309, fat 22 g, carbs 4.5 g, protein 24 g, sodium 1228 mg

Pork Chop Brussels Sprout Skillet

This low carb skillet supper is delicious and simple. Perfect for a weekday meal at only 7g carbs per serving.

Serves 4 | Prep. time 10 minutes | Cooking Time 20–25 minutes

Ingredients
1 pound boneless or bone-in pork chops (4–5 chops)
1½ tablespoons olive oil
1 teaspoon sea salt (divided)
½ teaspoon pepper (divided)
⅔ cup chicken broth
1 teaspoon Dijon mustard
½ tablespoon balsamic vinegar
¼ cup unsweetened applesauce
¼ cup onion, minced
2 cloves garlic, minced
1¼ cups Brussels sprouts, halved
1 tablespoon rosemary
1 tablespoon fresh sage leaves, chopped
2 slices bacon, cooked and crumbled

Directions
1. Heat a large skillet over medium to high heat, then add 1 tablespoon of olive oil.
2. Add the pork chops and season with salt and pepper. Cook on each side for about 6 minutes or until the chops are nicely browned, then remove them from the skillet.
3. Add the remaining oil to the skillet and then add the onion, garlic, Brussels sprouts, rosemary, and sage. Stir and let cook for about 5 minutes.
4. Mix together the broth, Dijon mustard, balsamic vinegar and applesauce with some salt and pepper.

5. Transfer the pork chops back to the skillet and pour the chicken broth mixture over them. Sprinkle with bacon and let cook for about 8 minutes.

Nutrition (per serving)
Calories 387, fat 22 g, carbs 7 g, protein 33 g, sodium 1044 mg

Instant Pot Chile Verde

This recipe is super simple, but it holds those amazing flavors you usually only get in a slow cooker. In fact, you *can* slow cook this recipe if you choose.

Serves 4 | Prep. time 10 minutes| Cooking time 40 minutes

Ingredients
2 pounds pork shoulder, cut into 6 pieces (or use pre-cut pork stew meat)
1½ tablespoons olive oil
1 teaspoon sea salt
½ teaspoon black pepper
1½ cups salsa verde
1½ cups chicken broth

Directions
1. Season the pork shoulder with salt and pepper.
2. Set your Instant Pot to sauté and add the olive oil. When the oil is hot, add the pork pieces and brown to sear in the juices.
3. When the meat has browned, pour the salsa verde and chicken broth into the Instant Pot and stir to cover the meat.
4. Place the cover on the pot and seal securely. Cook on high pressure for 40 minutes.
5. Let the cooker naturally release the pressure for 10 minutes, then manually release the rest of the pressure.
6. Shred the meat with two forks, stir to make sure it soaks in the delicious flavors of the sauce, and serve.

Nutrition (per serving)
Calories 342, fat 22 g, carbs 6 g, protein 32 g, sodium 710 mg

Italian Sausage and Kale Soup (Instant Pot)

You'll love this low carb soup when the weather turns cold. With only 8g carbs per serving, you can enjoy it often.

Serves 4 | Prep. time 5 minutes | Cooking time 30 minutes

Ingredients
1 cup onion, diced
6 cloves garlic, minced
1 pound hot Italian sausage, casing removed
12 ounces frozen cauliflower
12 ounces frozen kale
3 cups water
½ cup heavy whipping cream
½ cup shredded parmesan cheese for serving

Directions
1. Set your Instant Pot to sauté. When hot, add the sausage. Crumble and brown. Then add the onion and garlic and cook 2 minutes, stirring to get everything mixed.
2. Add the cauliflower, kale, and water.
3. Seal the Instant Pot and cook on high pressure for 3 minutes.
4. Let the pressure release naturally for 5 minutes, then manually release the rest.
5. Open the pot and stir to smash up the cauliflower (which will help thicken the soup). Slowly add the cream while continuing to stir.
6. Serve with parmesan cheese.

Nutrition (per serving)
Calories 400, fat 33 g, carbs 8 g, protein 16 g, sodium 827 mg

Lamb Goulash

This low carb recipe is hearty and rich. The lamb offers an alternative to beef and still keeps the carb count low.

Serves 8–10 | Prep. time 15 minutes | Cooking time 30 minutes

Ingredients
1 tablespoon olive oil
2 pounds ground lamb
1 yellow onion, diced
4 large cloves garlic, minced
1 (15-ounce) can tomato sauce
1 (14½-ounce) can diced tomatoes
1½ tablespoons soy sauce
2 tablespoons dried oregano
2 teaspoons dried basil
2 dried bay leaves
1 tablespoon seasoned salt
½ teaspoon black pepper
10 ounces cabbage, shredded
Cheddar Cheese, shredded (optional, for topping)

Directions
1. In a large skillet, heat the oil over medium to high heat. Add the lamb and brown, then add the onion and garlic.
2. Cook until the meat is no longer pink and the onions are soft.
3. Add the tomato sauce, diced tomatoes, soy sauce, oregano, basil, bay leaves, salt, and pepper. Heat to a gentle boil.
4. Turn the heat to low, cover and cook for 20 minutes.
5. Stir in the cabbage and let cook for an additional 5 minutes.
6. Remove the bay leaves and serve with cheddar cheese.

Nutrition (per serving)
Calories 222, fat 15 g, carbs 6 g, protein 14 g, sodium 964 mg

Fish & Seafood

Sheet Pan Eggs and Smoked Salmon

This easy baked egg dish with smoked salmon is a perfect meal to serve for breakfast, lunch or dinner.

Serves 12 | Prep. time 15 minutes | Cooking time 15 minutes

Ingredients
1½ tablespoons unsalted butter at room temperature
12 eggs
⅓ cup whole milk
Salt and freshly ground black pepper
¼ cup fresh dill, chopped (divided)
1½ cups smoked salmon, chopped
½ cup cream cheese
½ red onion, minced
3 tablespoons capers

Directions
1. Preheat the oven to 300°F.
2. In a large mixing bowl, whisk together the eggs, milk, salt, and pepper. Add in half of the fresh dill.
3. Transfer the eggs to a baking pan you have sprayed with cooking spray.
4. Place the smoked salmon evenly throughout the eggs along with dollops of cream cheese. Sprinkle red onion over the top. Transfer the pan to the oven and bake for approximately 15 minutes or until the eggs are set.
5. Garnish with capers and additional dill and serve.

Nutrition (per serving)
Calories 134, fat 10 g, carbs 2 g, protein 9 g, sodium 1116 mg

Pesto Salmon Milano

This aromatic salmon dish is full of flavor but easy to prepare and very low in carbs.

Serves 6 | Prep. time 10 minutes | Cooking time 20 minutes

Ingredients
2½ pounds large salmon fillets
½ cup basil pesto
½ cup butter, melted
2 medium tomatoes, sliced

Directions
1. Preheat the oven to 400°F.
2. Lay aluminum foil over the top of a baking sheet. Make the foil long enough that you'll be able to fold it over.
3. Lay the salmon fillets over the foil. Spread with pesto sauce and drizzle with melted butter.
4. Top with tomato slices and then pull up the foil to make a tent over the salmon. You may have to add another sheet of foil if it turns out the first sheet wasn't big enough.
5. Transfer to the oven and bake for 15–20 minutes. Flake fish with a fork to test for doneness. The salmon should easily come apart when it is done.

Nutrition (per serving)
Calories 449, fat 31 g, carbs 4 g, protein 37 g, sodium 483 mg

Roasted Lemon Pepper Salmon and Asparagus

Super tasty salmon with garlic parmesan asparagus is a fabulous way to create a memorable meal.

Serves 4 | Prep. time 10 minutes | Cooking time 20 minutes

Ingredients
1½ pounds salmon, skin on
2½ tablespoons olive oil (divided)
1 teaspoon lemon zest
1 tablespoon fresh lemon juice
4 cloves garlic, minced (divided)
1 teaspoon Dijon mustard
¾ teaspoon onion powder
½ teaspoon each salt and fresh cracked black pepper, plus more for asparagus
½ lemon, thinly sliced (optional)
1½–2 pounds asparagus, tough ends trimmed
½ cup parmesan, finely shredded

Directions
1. Preheat the oven to 400°F.
2. Line a baking sheet with parchment paper.
3. Place the salmon in the center of the baking sheet on top of the parchment paper.
4. In a small bowl, mix 1½ tablespoons of olive oil with the lemon zest, lemon juice, garlic, Dijon mustard, and onion powder. Stir with a fork to make sure that everything is well incorporated.
5. Using a pastry brush, brush the sauce over the salmon. Season with salt and pepper.

6. Line the asparagus up on either side of the salmon and brush with olive oil. Season it with salt and pepper and finish by sprinkling on the parmesan cheese.
7. Top the salmon with lemon slices and transfer it to the oven.
8. Bake for 10 minutes or until the salmon flakes easily with a fork.

Nutrition (per serving)
Calories 384, fat 23 g, carbs 3 g, protein 39 g, sodium 281 mg

Irish Whiskey Glazed Salmon

This is a fantastic recipe! Bursting with flavor and made in one pot, it's absolutely delicious and has only 2g carbs per serving.

Serves 6 | Prep. time 5 minutes | Cooking time 15 minutes

Ingredients
3 tablespoons butter
2 pounds salmon fillets, skin on, de-boned
1 teaspoon sea salt
1 teaspoon pepper
¼ cup garlic, diced
2 cups green beans, trimmed
½ cup Irish whiskey
1 cup heavy cream
¼ cup parsley to garnish

Directions
1. In a large nonstick skillet, melt the butter over medium-high heat.
2. Once the butter starts to get a bit foamy, add the salmon to the pan, skinless side down. Then add the garlic and the beans.
3. Cook for 4 minutes or until the garlic starts to brown and become fragrant.
4. Flip the salmon over so that the skin side is down. Be careful you don't break it. A large spatula should work well.
5. Pour in the whiskey. You can light the whiskey on fire with a long match, which will remove some of the alcohol and the strong flavor, but you don't have to. If you do, wait until the flame goes out before proceeding to the next step.

6. Turn off the heat and gently move the salmon to one side of the pan.
7. Slowly pour in the cream, whisking so that it blends with the whiskey. Turn the heat back on to medium and cook the salmon until it flakes easily with a fork.
8. Remove the salmon and beans to a serving dish, turn the heat up to high, and let the sauce boil for a couple of minutes to reduce.
9. Serve the salmon with the sauce over the top.

Nutrition (per serving)
Calories 680, fat 45 g, carbs 2 g, protein 46 g, sodium 782 mg

Garlic Shrimp Asparagus Skillet

Garlic, shrimp, and asparagus combine to create an amazingly delicious dish that you will want to eat every night!

Serves 4 | Prep. time 10 minutes | Cooking time 10–15 minutes

Ingredients
1 pound uncooked extra-large shrimp, peeled
Kosher salt and freshly ground black pepper to taste
Pinch of crushed red pepper or red pepper flakes
1 teaspoon onion powder
3 tablespoons extra-virgin olive oil (divided)
3 cloves garlic, minced
2 cups mushroom, sliced
1 bunch asparagus, ends trimmed and cut in halves
1 tablespoon fresh parsley, chopped

Directions
1. To a medium mixing bowl, add the shrimp, salt, pepper, and onion powder. Stir to ensure that the shrimp is seasoned well.
2. In a large skillet, heat 2 tablespoons of the olive oil over medium heat.
3. Add the garlic and cook for 1 minute or until the garlic smells fragrant.
4. Add the shrimp to the skillet and cook until the shrimp loses its translucent look. Remove the shrimp from the skillet.
5. Add the remaining olive oil to the skillet and heat it. Then add the asparagus and mushrooms, cooking until the asparagus is fork tender.
6. Return the shrimp to the pan and stir to combine.

Nutrition (per serving)
Calories 187, fat 9 g, carbs 8 g, protein 20 g, sodium 233 mg

Mediterranean Baked Cod

This cod recipe is so simple, yet it has such wonderful flavor. It is also low in calories, carbs, and fat.

Serves 4 | Prep. time 5 minutes | Cooking time 15 minutes

Ingredients
1 medium onion, thinly sliced
6 ounces mini sweet peppers
½ teaspoon salt
1 tablespoon extra-virgin olive oil
1 pint grape tomatoes, halved
8 sprigs fresh thyme
1½ pounds cod fillets
¼ cup water
½ teaspoon pepper

Directions
1. Preheat oven to 450°F.
2. In an ovenproof skillet or Dutch oven, heat the olive oil over medium-high heat on the stovetop.
3. When the oil is hot, add in the onions, peppers, and salt. Cook until the onions are soft.
4. Add the tomatoes and thyme to the skillet along with some additional salt and pepper. Cook for 2 minutes. Add the cod fillets and the water. Cover the skillet, transfer it to the oven, and bake for 15 minutes.
5. Serve with the thyme leaves as decoration, or remove them completely.

Nutrition (per serving)
Calories 205, fat 5 g, carbs 8 g, protein 32 g, sodium 115 mg

Instant Pot Tilapia with Spinach

This Instant Pot recipe is easy to prepare and makes a great freezer recipe for a make-ahead meal.

Serves 4 | Prep. time 10 minutes | Cooking time 5 minutes

Ingredients
2 cups mushrooms, chopped
2 cups tomatoes, diced
2 cups spinach, chopped
¾ cup fresh basil, chopped
¾ cup parsley, chopped
3 teaspoons garlic, minced
3 tablespoons olive oil
¼ cup lime juice
½ teaspoon lime zest
½ teaspoon salt
½ teaspoon black pepper
1 pound tilapia
1 cup water

Directions
1. In a mixing bowl, combine the mushrooms, tomatoes, and spinach, then add in the basil, parsley, garlic, olive oil, lime juice, and lime zest.
2. Place the tilapia on individual pieces of aluminum foil and season with salt and pepper.
3. Add some of the spinach mixture to the top of each fish fillet, then fold the foil over to form a package.
4. Place the trivet in the bottom of your Instant Pot and add the cup of water.
5. Place the foil packets on top of the trivet and securely seal the Instant Pot.

6. Cook the fish on high pressure for 5 minutes, then manually release the pressure.
7. Remove from the packets and serve.

Nutrition (per serving)
Calories 250, fat 13 g, carbs 8 g, protein 26 g, sodium 410 mg

Tilapia Vera Cruz

This super simple 5-ingredient fish meal has only 4g carbs per serving as well as only 50 calories!

Serves 4 | Prep. time 10 minutes | Cooking time 12 minutes

Ingredients
4 6-ounce fillets tilapia or other mild white fish
1 cup salsa
¼ cup Spanish olives, sliced
1 cup broccoli florets or zucchini, sliced
½ tablespoon olive oil
1 teaspoon kosher salt
1 lime, juice and zest
½ cup cilantro, chopped

Directions
1. In a medium skillet, heat the oil and then sauté the broccoli or zucchini until it begins to soften.
2. Season the tilapia with a bit of salt and pepper and place it in the skillet. Cook on one side for 3 minutes, then flip to the other side, taking care not to break the fillets.
3. Add in the salsa, olives and lime zest and continue cooking for 6 minutes or until the fish flakes easily with a fork.
4. Before serving, pour the lime juice over the top and garnish with cilantro.

Nutrition (per serving)
Calories 47, fat 3 g, carbs 4 g, protein 1 g, sodium 1172 mg

Vegetarian

Mediterranean Zucchini Noodle Pasta

Garlicky, butter noodles and still low in carbs. Who needs carbs? A lot of grocery stores are selling zucchini noodles in the produce section if you don't have a spiral slicer.

Serves 4 | Prep. time 10 minutes | Cooking time 10 minutes

Ingredients
2 large zucchinis, spiral sliced
1 cup spinach, packed
2 tablespoons olive oil
2 tablespoons butter
5 cloves garlic, minced
Sea salt and black pepper to taste
¼ cup sundried tomatoes
2 tablespoons capers
2 tablespoons Italian flat leaf parsley, chopped
10 Kalamata olives, halved
¼ cup Parmesan cheese, shredded
¼ cup feta cheese, crumbled

Directions
1. In a large skillet, heat the olive oil. When the oil is hot, add the zucchini, spinach, butter, garlic, salt, and pepper and cook until the spinach gets soft.
2. There may be extra liquid; if so, drain it off.
3. Add in the sundried tomatoes, capers, parsley, and olives. Mix well and let cook for just a minute or two more.
4. Serve with parmesan and feta cheese.

Nutrition (per serving)
Calories 231, fat 20 g, carbs 6.5 g, protein 6.5 g, sodium 509 mg

Spinach and Feta Pie

This classic dish makes a wonderful supper any night of the week. At less than 5g carbs per serving, you will love it even more.

Serves 6 | Prep. time 10 minutes | Cooking time 40 minutes

Ingredients
1 pound spinach, fresh or frozen
6 medium eggs, beaten
½ onion, finely diced
1 cup full-fat cream cheese
8 ounces feta cheese, crumbled
Huge handful fresh mint, chopped
Salt and pepper to taste

Directions
1. Preheat oven to 350°F.
2. If you are using frozen spinach, defrost it, put it in a very small-holed colander, and smash out all the water. If you are using fresh spinach, chop it and cook it briefly in a skillet or the microwave to wilt it, then drain out any liquid.
3. Mix all of the ingredients together in a mixing bowl. Make sure the cream cheese is mixed in. You may want to mix the feta in last to leave bits of it whole.
4. Pour the contents of the mixing bowl into a pie plate that has been buttered or sprayed with cooking spray.
5. Bake for 40 minutes or until the eggs are set.

Nutrition (per serving)
Calories 209, fat 16 g, carbs 4.2 g, protein 10.6 g, sodium 725 mg

Portobello Pizza

This pizza recipe utilizes the perfect pocket of a Portobello mushroom so you don't have to worry about a crust.

Serves 4 | Prep. time 10 minutes | Cooking time 20 minutes

Ingredients
Olive oil spray
4 large Portobello mushrooms
½ cup marinara sauce
½ cup shredded mozzarella
½ cup peppers, diced
½ cup cheddar, shredded

Directions
1. Preheat the oven to 375°F.
2. Spray a baking sheet with olive oil spray.
3. Scrape out the insides of the Portobello mushrooms.
4. Put the mushrooms on the baking sheet and fill them with the marinara, peppers, and cheeses. (You can add any other vegetables you want, but that may change the carb count.)
5. Bake for 20 minutes or until the cheese is melted and starting to brown.

Nutrition (per serving)
Calories 113, fat 6 g, carbs 5 g, protein 7 g, sodium 368 mg

Cauliflower Fried Rice

This low carb take on a traditional dish is easy to prepare, and your taste buds will never notice the missing rice. Many grocery stores sell riced cauliflower in the produce section to save you the very short time it takes to rice it yourself.

Serves 6 | Prep. time 5 minutes | Cooking time 15 minutes

Ingredients
3 tablespoons butter (divided)
2 cloves garlic, minced
½ large onion, finely diced
½ medium red pepper, finely diced
2 large eggs
Sea salt
Black pepper
1 medium head cauliflower (or 4 cups riced cauliflower)
2 tablespoons coconut aminos or soy sauce
1 teaspoon toasted sesame oil
3 medium green onions, chopped

Directions
1. Rice the cauliflower (unless you've bought the cauliflower already riced).
2. In a large skillet, melt 2 tablespoons of butter. Add the garlic, onion, and red peppers. Cook until the onions and peppers are soft.
3. In a separate bowl, beat the eggs with some salt and pepper.
4. Move the veggies over to the side of the skillet and cook the egg for a minute or so, until it is lightly scrambled.
5. Move the egg over with the veggies and melt the remaining butter. Then add the rice and stir everything together. Cook for about 5 more minutes.
6. Season with salt and pepper and serve.

Nutrition (per serving)
Calories 127, fat 8 g, carbs 6 g, protein 5 g, sodium 471 mg

Cheese Cauliflower Casserole

This recipe couldn't be any easier to prepare but is so full of flavor it will taste like you spent all day cooking. A taste of Italy without the carbs.

Serves 8 | Prep. time 5 minutes | Cooking time 35 minutes

Ingredients
8 cups cooked cauliflower florets, well drained
2 cups pasta sauce
2 tablespoons heavy whipping cream
2 tablespoons melted butter
⅓ cup parmesan cheese, grated
½ teaspoon kosher salt
¼ teaspoon ground black pepper
6 slices provolone cheese
¼ cup fresh basil, chopped

Directions
1. Preheat oven to 375°F.
2. In a large mixing bowl, thoroughly mix together the cauliflower, vodka sauce, cream, butter, parmesan, salt, and pepper.
3. Pour the mixture into a 9×13 baking pan and top with the provolone cheese slices.
4. Transfer to the oven and bake for 35 minutes or until the cheese is melted and bubbly.
5. Serve with basil.

Nutrition (per serving)
Calories 214, fat 14 g, carbs 6 g, protein 12 g, sodium 884 mg

Cooked Eggplant Salad

This is a simple recipe that is full of rich flavors and low in carbohydrates. The eggplant is healthy and the salad is very filling.

Serves 4–6 | Prep. time 15 minutes | Cooking time 1 hour

Ingredients
2 large eggplants, peeled and cubed
6 tablespoons olive oil
2 red or yellow bell peppers, seeded and cut into chunks
4 cloves garlic, minced
1 (15-ounce) can tomato sauce
1 cup water
1 teaspoon cumin
1 teaspoon salt (or to taste)
1 teaspoon sugar
½ teaspoon crushed red pepper flakes
¼ teaspoon black pepper

Directions
1. To a stockpot, add 3 tablespoons of olive oil and the eggplant. Let the eggplant cook up a bit, browning slightly.
2. If necessary, add the remaining olive oil. Add the peppers and garlic and allow them to cook for another couple of minutes or until the peppers soften and the garlic becomes fragrant.
3. In a small bowl, combine the tomato sauce, water, cumin, sugar, salt, pepper, and red pepper flakes. Stir to combine, then add to the pot with the eggplant and peppers.
4. Reduce the heat to low and allow to simmer for about 1 hour or until the mixture thickens and the sauce is reduced.

Nutrition (per serving)
Calories 99, fat 7 g, carbs 8 g, protein 1 g, sodium 384 mg

Spinach Artichoke Casserole

This recipe turns spinach artichoke dip into a delicious low carb casserole that you will love.

Serves 4 | Prep. time 10 minutes | Cooking time 6 hours

Ingredients
8 large eggs
¾ cup unsweetened almond milk
5 ounces fresh spinach, chopped
6 ounces artichoke hearts, chopped (thaw and drain if frozen, drain if marinated)
1 cup parmesan, grated
3 cloves garlic, minced
1 teaspoon salt
½ teaspoon pepper
¾ cup coconut flour
1 tablespoon baking powder

Directions
1. Spray the inside of your slow cooker with cooking spray.
2. In a mixing bowl, beat together the eggs, milk, spinach, artichokes, ½ cup of the parmesan cheese, garlic, salt, and pepper.
3. Whisk in the coconut flour and baking powder until well incorporated.
4. Cover the slow cooker and cook on high for 2–3 hours or low for 6 hours.

Nutrition (per serving)
Calories 141, fat 7.1 g, carbs 7.7 g, protein 9.8 g, sodium 515 mg

Zucchini Casserole

This cheesy casserole will please every member of your family. It is low and carbs and easy to prepare.

Serves 6 | Prep. time 10 minutes | Cooking time 30 minutes

Ingredients
3 medium zucchinis, sliced into ¼-inch-thick slices, washed and dried
Sea salt
Black pepper
1½ cup Gruyere shredded cheese blend (or any shredded sharp cheese; divided)
3 ounces Brie cheese (edges cut off)
⅓ cup heavy cream
2 tablespoons unsweetened almond milk
1 tablespoon butter
2 cloves garlic, minced or crushed
½ tablespoon Italian seasoning

Directions
1. Preheat oven to 400°F.
2. Arrange the zucchini in a baking dish. You can either make rows with the slices or make a couple of layers. Sprinkle some of the shredded cheese over the zucchini and season with salt and pepper.
3. To a small bowl, add the Brie, cream, almond milk and butter. Microwave for 30 seconds at a time until the cheese melts and it is smooth. Don't let it boil or the cream may get an odd texture. When it is ready, pour over the zucchini and then add a layer of the remaining shredded cheese and sprinkle with the Italian seasoning.
4. Bake for 30–35 minutes or until bubbly.

Nutrition (per serving)
Calories 1239, fat 19 g, carbs 6 g, protein 12 g, sodium 669 mg

Desserts

Flourless Chocolate Peanut Butter Cake

Chocolate and peanut butter together, does it need any explanation? Oh yeah, there are only 5g carbs a serving!

Serves 1 | Prep. time 5 minutes | Cooking time 1 minute 20 seconds

Ingredients
2 tablespoons unsweetened cocoa powder
2 tablespoons erythritol
1 large egg
1 tablespoon heavy cream
½ teaspoon vanilla extract
¼ teaspoon baking powder
1 teaspoon salted butter
1 tablespoon peanut butter

Directions
1. In a small bowl, mix the cocoa powder, sweetener and baking powder together with a fork. Make sure to get rid of any lumps.
2. In another small bowl, mix together the wet ingredients, then combine these with the cocoa powder mixture.
3. Use butter to grease a small ramekin or mug. Pour in the batter and microwave for 1 minute and 20 seconds.
4. Serve with a dollop of the peanut butter, or you can melt the peanut butter in the microwave and pour it over the top.

Nutrition (per serving)
Calories 246, fat 20 g, carbs 5 g, protein 10 g, sodium 96 mg

Peanut Butter Nice Cream

Ice cream that's low carb? Yep. It's super easy to prepare, and you will love the flavor.

Serves 6–8 | Prep. time 5 minutes | Cooking time 15 minutes

Ingredients
1 (13½-ounce) can full-fat coconut milk
½ cup peanut butter (creamy, no sugar added)
⅓ cup coconut oil (measured solid, then melted)
¼ cup cocoa powder
½ cup powdered erythritol (or any powdered sweetener)
Pinch sea salt (optional)

Directions
1. Dump all of the ingredients into a food processor and puree until smooth.
2. Pour into a freezer-proof container and freeze for 30 minutes, then take it out and stir it up. Put it back in the freezer and freeze for 3 hours or overnight.

Nutrition (per serving)
Calories 362, fat 35 g, carbs 8 g, protein 6 g, sodium 34 mg

Pressure Cooker Pumpkin Pudding

This dessert is absolutely scrumptious, and it is totally carb friendly and easy to make in your Instant Pot.

Serves 6 | Prep. time 10 minutes | Cooking time 30 minutes

Ingredients
2 eggs
½ cup heavy whipping cream (or almond milk for dairy-free)
¾ cup erythritol (or sweetener of choice such as Swerve, Truvia or Splenda)
1 (15-ounce) can pumpkin puree
1 teaspoon pumpkin pie spice
1 teaspoon vanilla
½ cup heavy whipping cream, whipped with a mixer, for serving

Directions
1. In a mixing bowl, beat together the eggs, then the cream, then the sweetener, then the pumpkin, then the spice and finally the vanilla.
2. Pour the pumpkin mixture into a greased 6×3 round cake pan and cover with aluminum foil.
3. Put the steamer rack in the Instant Pot and add 1½ cups of water.
4. Place the pan with the pudding mixture on the steamer rack.
5. Secure the lid on the Instant Pot and cook on high for 20 minutes. Let the pressure release naturally for 10 minutes, then release the rest manually.
6. Remove the lid carefully, making sure you don't allow any of the water that will have condensed on the bottom of the lid to fall into the pudding.
7. Chill the pudding for 6–8 hours, then serve with the whipped cream.

Nutrition (per serving)
Calories 184, fat 16 g, carbs 8 g, protein 3 g, sodium 104 mg

Slow Cooker Mocha Pudding Cake

This amazing pudding cake will have everyone in the family begging you to make it again!

Serves 6| Prep. time 10 minutes | Cooking time 2–3 hours

Ingredients
¾ cup butter, cut into large chunks
2 ounces unsweetened chocolate, finely chopped
½ cup heavy cream
2 tablespoons instant coffee crystals
1 teaspoon vanilla extract
¼ cup unsweetened cocoa powder
⅓ cup almond flour
⅛ teaspoon salt
5 large eggs
⅔ cup stevia/erythritol granulated sweetener

Directions
1. Spray your slow cooker with cooking spray.
2. In a small bowl, mix together the cream, coffee, and vanilla.
3. Melt the chocolate and butter in the microwave in 20-second increments until smooth.
4. In another bowl, combine the cocoa powder, flour, and salt. Mix well.
5. Using a hand mixer, mix the eggs and the sweetener together until frothy, then add in the melted chocolate, then the cream mixture.
6. Pour the batter into the slow cooker and cook on low for 2–3 hours.

Nutrition (per serving)
Calories 413, fat 39 g, carbs 3.7 g, protein 9.3 g, sodium 141 mg

Coconut Almond Cake

This delicious cake is done in the blink of an eye and is carb friendly.

Serves 8 | Prep. time 10 minutes | Cooking time 40 minutes

Ingredients
1 cup almond flour
½ cup unsweetened shredded coconut
⅓ cup Truvia
1 teaspoon baking powder
1 teaspoon apple pie spice
2 eggs, lightly whisked
¼ cup butter, melted
½ cup heavy whipping cream

Directions
1. Mix together all of the dry ingredients in a large mixing bowl.
2. Slowly add in the eggs, then the butter, then the whipping cream, mixing until there are no lumps.
3. Pour the mixture into a round cake pan that has been sprayed with nonstick cooking spray. Cover the pan with foil.
4. Place the steamer rack in your Instant Pot or pressure cooker and add 1½ cups of water.
5. Place the cake pan on the steamer rack and securely attach the lid.
6. Cook on high pressure for 40 minutes and let the pressure release naturally for 10 minutes. Manually release the rest of the pressure. When you remove the lid, be careful not to let any water drop on the cake.
7. Serve garnished with extra coconut if desired.

Nutrition (per serving)
Calories 236, fat 11 g, carbs 5 g, protein 5 g, sodium 66 mg

Instant Pot Lemon Cheesecake

This Instant Pot cheesecake with the deliciously light tang of lemon will surely be a family favorite.

Serves 6 | Prep. time 10 minutes | Cooking Time 30 minutes

Ingredients
1 cup cream cheese
¼ cup Truvia
⅓ cup ricotta cheese
1 lemon, zest and juice
½ teaspoon lemon extract
2 eggs
Topping
2 tablespoons sour cream
1 teaspoon Truvia

Directions
1. Mix all of the cheesecake ingredients but the eggs together with a mixer until smooth.
2. With a fork, gently beat in the eggs just until they are well blended.
3. Pour the mixture into a pan that has been sprayed with cooking spray. It is easiest to use a springform pan, but if you don't have one a relatively deep round cake pan will work. Whichever you use, cover it with foil.
4. Put the steamer rack in your Instant Pot and add 1½ cups of water. Set the pan on the steamer rack. Secure the lid and cook on high pressure for 30 minutes.
5. Let the pressure release naturally.
6. If you want to use the sour cream topping, wait until the cake has cooled, then mix the sour cream and sweetener together. You can serve with a dollop on each slice or frost the cake, whichever you prefer.

Nutrition (per serving)
Calories 181, fat 9 g, carbs 2 g, protein 5 g, sodium 245 mg

Blackberry Cobbler

With this recipe, you can have delicious blackberry cobbler and not feel guilty as there are only 7g carbs per serving.

Serves 8 | Prep. time 10 minutes | Cooking time 25 minutes

Ingredients
1 pound blackberries
2 tablespoons lemon juice
⅓ cup erythritol sweetener blend (or ¼ cup if you want it less sweet)
2 tablespoons gelatin
Cobbler Topping
1 cup almond flour
3 tablespoons monk fruit/erythritol sweetener blend
½ teaspoon baking powder
¼ teaspoon sea salt
¼ cup coconut oil or butter, melted
½ teaspoon vanilla extract

Directions
1. Preheat oven to 350°F.
2. In a mixing bowl, stir together the blackberries, lemon juice, and sweetener, then add in 1 tablespoon at a time of the gelatin, stirring to ensure it is equally distributed. Pour the berries into a nonstick baking pan.
3. In a large bowl, mix together the topping ingredients. Combine until crumbly then spread over the top of the berries.
4. Transfer the pan to the oven and bake for 30 minutes or until the topping turns a nice golden brown and you can see the berries bubbling underneath.

Nutrition (per serving)
Calories 154, fat 12 g, carbs 7 g, protein 5 g, sodium 71 mg

Lemon Cheesecake Fluff

This recipe is extremely easy and there is no baking. Just whip it together, put it in the refrigerator for a bit, and voila! Dessert with only 5g carbs per serving.

Serves 4 | Prep. time 5 minutes

Ingredients
8 ounces cream cheese
½ cup heavy whipping cream
3 tablespoons lemon juice
¼ teaspoon salt
2 teaspoons pure vanilla extract
1 tablespoon erythritol (optional)

Directions
1. In a large bowl, beat together the cream cheese and the whipping cream until fluffy.
2. Beat in the lemon juice, salt, and vanilla. Taste. If you prefer it a little sweeter, add the sweetener.
3. You can transfer the mixture to individual dishes at this point, or just put the mixing bowl in the refrigerator for at least 30 minutes before serving. Enjoy!

Nutrition (per serving)
Calories 310, fat 30 g, carbs 5 g, protein 4 g, sodium 103 mg

Recipe Index

Chicken & Poultry _____ 3
   Chicken and Veggies _____ 3
   Slow Cooker Chicken and Bacon Chowder _____ 4
   Chicken Jalapeno Popper Soup _____ 5
   Kung Pao Chicken _____ 7
   Chicken Marsala _____ 9
   White Chicken Chili _____ 10
   Chicken Cordon Bleu Casserole _____ 11
   Bacon Ranch Chicken _____ 13
   Creamy Spinach Artichoke Chicken _____ 14
   Sheet Pan Fajitas _____ 15
Beef _____ 17
   Beef, Spinach and Mozzarella Bake _____ 17
   Corned Beef Hash _____ 19
   Cheesy Taco Soup _____ 20
   Instant Pot Beef Bourguignon _____ 21
   Stuffed Meatloaf _____ 23
   Slow Cooker Beef Stroganoff _____ 24
   Instant Pot Boneless Short Ribs _____ 25
   Thai Lettuce Wraps with Veal _____ 27
Pork & Lamb _____ 29
   Slow Cooked Lamb with Mint and Green Beans _____ 29
   Crock Pot Ham Cauliflower "Potato" Soup _____ 30
   Pork Egg Roll in a Bowl _____ 31
   Pizza Frittata _____ 32
   Pork Chop Brussels Sprout Skillet _____ 33
   Instant Pot Chile Verde _____ 35
   Italian Sausage and Kale Soup (Instant Pot) _____ 36
   Lamb Goulash _____ 37

- Fish & Seafood — 39
  - Sheet Pan Eggs and Smoked Salmon — 39
  - Pesto Salmon Milano — 40
  - Roasted Lemon Pepper Salmon and Asparagus — 41
  - Irish Whiskey Glazed Salmon — 43
  - Garlic Shrimp Asparagus Skillet — 45
  - Mediterranean Baked Cod — 46
  - Instant Pot Tilapia with Spinach — 47
  - Tilapia Vera Cruz — 49
- Vegetarian — 51
  - Mediterranean Zucchini Noodle Pasta — 51
  - Spinach and Feta Pie — 52
  - Portobello Pizza — 53
  - Cauliflower Fried Rice — 54
  - Cheese Cauliflower Casserole — 55
  - Cooked Eggplant Salad — 56
  - Spinach Artichoke Casserole — 57
  - Zucchini Casserole — 58
- Desserts — 59
  - Flourless Chocolate Peanut Butter Cake — 59
  - Peanut Butter Nice Cream — 60
  - Pressure Cooker Pumpkin Pudding — 61
  - Slow Cooker Mocha Pudding Cake — 62
  - Coconut Almond Cake — 63
  - Instant Pot Lemon Cheesecake — 64
  - Blackberry Cobbler — 65
  - Lemon Cheesecake Fluff — 66

Also by Sarah Spencer

Appendix - Cooking Conversion Charts

1. Measuring Equivalent Chart

Type	Imperial	Imperial	Metric
Weight	1 dry ounce		28g
	1 pound	16 dry ounces	0.45 kg
Volume	1 teaspoon		5 ml
	1 dessert spoon	2 teaspoons	10 ml
	1 tablespoon	3 teaspoons	15 ml
	1 Australian tablespoon	4 teaspoons	20 ml
	1 fluid ounce	2 tablespoons	30 ml
	1 cup	16 tablespoons	240 ml
	1 cup	8 fluid ounces	240 ml
	1 pint	2 cups	470 ml
	1 quart	2 pints	0.95 l
	1 gallon	4 quarts	3.8 l
Length	1 inch		2.54 cm

* Numbers are rounded to the closest equivalent

2. Oven Temperature Equivalent Chart

Fahrenheit (°F)	Celsius (°C)	Gas Mark
220	100	
225	110	1/4
250	120	1/2
275	140	1
300	150	2
325	160	3
350	180	4
375	190	5
400	200	6
425	220	7
450	230	8
475	250	9
500	260	

* Celsius (°C) = T (°F)-32] * 5/9
** Fahrenheit (°F) = T (°C) * 9/5 + 32
*** Numbers are rounded to the closest equivalent

Made in United States
Troutdale, OR
09/21/2023